I soaked up these poems like a charac... ...ohn Cheever story. I dove into them as i... ... enchanted David Hockney swimming pool painting. Samuel Amadon immerses you in the "advanced fantasies" of a silver-tongued poet. Meaning is never exactly narrative. It's saturated with vernacular fluency, lyrical acuity, expressive idiosyncrasy. You simply have to read this fascinating book to grasp its mercurial energies, its enigmatic clarity. *Often, Common, Some, And Free* is remarkable and wonderfully irreducible.

**TERRANCE HAYES**

author of *American Sonnets for My Past and Future Assassin*

The figure who wanders the streets of New York, in Amadon's latest book, can't help but see, behind every edifice—including his own self—the demolition required to build any site. Welded by reverie and hypotheses, enjambment and psychogeography, these lyrics act less like frozen music, as composed by Robert Moses, than scaffolding. Reading them is akin to sandblasting a façade while treading a relay of boards, casually vertiginous and "belilaced" by a botany of asphalt and human sprawl. Their logic and syntax are potholed and cracked, coaxing us to look down, as well as up, as we follow no map. Taxis and swimming pools, turnstiles and bridges, lovers in coffee shops: "the city is an idea," our guide proposes, continuing where O'Hara and Oppen left off, an opening crossed by the mind and feet in sync, or syncopation. Now concerted, now astray, the score for this Gotham eclogue is a bewildering, weirdly infectious tinnitus, "ringing everywhere for me / too."

**ANDREW ZAWACKI**

author of *Unsun : f/11*

These poems Beatrice us into an infrastructure-past, natter us through a not-so-grand civic grandeur that's something like a citizenship stolen from us before we were ever born. You might want to chlorinate your feet after you break open this spine—it seems every genius has a red velvet swing to hide. Get your coffee to go.

**MAGDALENA ZURAWSKI**

author of *The Tiniest Muzzle Sings Songs of Freedom.*

OFTEN, COMMON,
SOME,
AND FREE

SAMUEL AMADON

# OFTEN, COMMON, SOME, AND FREE

## POEMS

OMNIDAWN
OAKLAND, CALIFORNIA
2021

Cover art: "Dark Duck," oil on jute, 94 x 68 inches, by Spencer Lewis, 2018
Photography by Ruben Diaz, courtesy of the artist

Cover typefaces: Tribute and Scala sans
Interior typefaces: Scala with Tribute and Scala sans

Cover and interior design by adam b. bohannon

Library of Congress Cataloging-in-Publication Data

Names: Amadon, Samuel, author.
Title: Often, common, some, and free / Samuel Amadon.
Description: Oakland, California : Omnidawn Publishing, 2021. | Summary:
"Often, Common, Some, And Free is a book about transformation. Moving
across varied formal and aesthetic terrain, these poems take on the
subject of literal change: constructing and tearing down physical
buildings, roaming between cities, and drawing together an image of a
world in flux. The speaker is in movement: walking, flying, swimming,
taking the train, while also constantly twisting in his sentences,
turning into different versions of himself, and braiding his voice with
others. These poems are interested in subjects that encompass creation
and loss from Robert Moses to the Gardner Museum robbery, but they aim
ultimately to resist destruction, to be in the particular, and to hold
still their world and their ever-shifting speaker"-- Provided by publisher.
Identifiers: LCCN 2021032524 | ISBN 9781632430946 (paperback)
Subjects: LCGFT: Poetry.
Classification: LCC PS3601.M33 O34 2021 | DDC 811/.6--dc23
LC record available at https://lccn.loc.gov/2021032524

Published by Omnidawn Publishing, Oakland, California
www.omnidawn.com    (510) 237-5472
10 9 8 7 6 5 4 3 2 1
ISBN: 978-1-63243-094-6

*for Liz Countryman*

# CONTENTS

# ONE

## POEM FOR THE OPENING OF THE HAMILTON FISH PARK POOL, 1936

A black cloud composed of cutouts of Moses
On the beam, Moses laughing, holding
A letter. We saw him first on a cool June evening,
While we entered the bathhouse, twenty-
Two hundred, and dipped our feet in basins of
Disinfectant so that the sky above the pavilions
Chlorinated with silver reflection. Or I was there
Almost alone, barely fit in my body and ready
To turn, to clarify as I descended, found I was able to
Descend. Things are overhead. Choruses
Of things turn around me. I am in a pool.
Robert Moses swims with me, and I with him.
I say: "Oh let the decades filter outward!"
And he says: "Let them file down the streets."

## A PARTIAL VIEW OF THE TRIBOROUGH

Ever since I was a boy, I've found
in names and personalities little
hints of interest, latches on the slightest
meaning. Not parlance. Let me say power.
The days rotate on their hinges. I can say I had
friends. Sizeable numbers, without delay, we were
like, I don't know, an absence. A civilization.
Prompt and unlike ourselves at all times: it was as if
we could stand to burst, to rapidly be
our own engines, rules, buildings, steel columns,
iron beams. This is when I said I had a foundry.
I had a scale, a summary and reflection, not
the desire, but the capacity to be
greater in titles and official things. Then I gave
it up. I sunk hillsides and fields and ash dumps.
I ran the concrete forth and I became the swarm,
the throng, corporate in absurdity. Most people
in opposition would say these are
the words I've prepared, while I am a speaker
without my text, let the day surprise me.
If it falls, it's me who gathers from idiosyncrasies
sentences to shape a state and city.

## POEM THAT WANTS TO BE CALLED THE WEST SIDE HIGHWAY

You can do the work just by starting it. You can
do whatever you want. A bill
is drafted on a train to Albany, or in a black
limousine. Like how one day I walked
the entire length of Manhattan, except I didn't.
I didn't finish. Not nearly. How could I?
Stopped as I was by the boat basin. These
credit cards fill with gin
and tonic. They pool with the stuff. Maybe
I get a little lost sometimes,
start thinking I went to Yale. Once I swam
to Governors Island, between the ferries
and freighters. It was like a job you should've seen
me quit. Maybe they looked for me. Maybe
it wasn't someone else's shift, and then
it was. Sometimes people are just turnstiles.
You have to tell them to keep
turning, keep turning into someone else. The rain
crashes across a cab, and the road
has filled. We're waterborne. Or whatever
the word is for that little moment
when the heart lifts. Why don't you devote
yourself the way you once did? It's
an old answer, and an early
one. The alarm goes off for a while after it
stops. In your face in the bathroom

mirror. You play that little song to look at
your teeth. My teeth. They haven't been cared for.
The class giggles at my age. This is
my hearing. The chances taken on a new face.

## THE BROOKLYN-BATTERY BRIDGE IN THE BROOKLYN-BATTERY TUNNEL

You might make a choice between what descends
with these tiles lined before you, or arcing
forward through a history that is constant against us.
A bridge to block out the dawn. Or monoxide
that passes like breath. My breath. I know all about what's
underground, and I keep my searches for the invisible
there. In the park above, you've got your bike locked
and the chain cut. The stubborn part doesn't say
anything, doesn't need to to
start marching home, ugly block, block of shouting, block
syrupy with flies. I would like to hear about it, but I am
backed into an argument myself
on a coil of cool fall breeze, backed through
seasons into the past, home or near it, in the moment
when I'm as right as I'll ever be bled into
I'll be this right forever. There's no out available
for this character, just a decade producing the present,
warm, and then warmer around him.
It was as if I hadn't seen the harbor, didn't want to
admit it by doing so now. Something
like a pile of books falls over inside me or
the room I'm in breaks off from the house, slides
almost out of view. All things didn't happen
or did. You might've routed a highway so it
crashes through the seventh floor of
a skyscraper, and the moment for that passes by
us still. You can live like a column of light
pours over you, but that's not all you'll see.

## VISIONARY LABORS OF THE ASTORIA POOL

He only likes to build it. He doesn't live
Where he swims, where the city has pieces,
He means to mend them, to tear the city
Pieces where it can be mended. Here
At my desk, I engage in a crisis among us.
What I'm doing is with my development.
What I'm doing these days is cutting out
The part I've done before. Done it for.
Our stability isn't in question if it's
Always in question. We can figure it out
From swimming, that we have to keep
Moving. Not just to float, but because
We can't help ourselves. It works like this:
I build what I see, and you try to stop me.

## ADVANCED FANTASIES OF THE CROSS-BRONX EXPRESSWAY

Here the Crotona Pool should be, here still
It is. We don't erase ourselves. We don't
Ply our bodies with asphalt and barriers.
Our walls are pinned with some of what
Exists, but one cannot notice every tulip,
All the flora and fauna given a name
Haven't been given one by us. The people
List as traffic. Thus traffic grows. It roars
When locked in place, then when it moves.
It piles around us, above us, like papers
We haven't attended to. We have too many
Solutions. Nights our offices pool with
Us. We overflow ourselves, and cannot
See from where we are about to go.

**SUNSET POOL**

Things are where we wanted them to be.
These cutouts—blue—on the city, spread
Like holes in the folds of a map: I walk
Into them, little frames of a sequence
In which I am a person touring swimming
Pools. Perhaps I feel something pass.
Perhaps I've begun to gather something
That seems elusive only because I can't
Turn away. At the base of this pool, empty
But for a pile of leaves and Robert Moses
Sliding out from under my reach—as I fall—
Slipping pool lights into my eyes: like crystals,
They color inside themselves, a blue which
Clears the second the light leaves them.

## AT MCCARREN POOL

Here I am with all the words
I didn't used to know. Here
Where cement and point
Collide, where the horizon

Falls off everything. It's odd
To be completely alone
With what you've made. All
The different orders

Handed out on slips of paper—
Or cupped against an ear—
So I'll never have them
Again. Messages passed, as in

This is a type, that a wave.
"Here a Roman arch,"
A Roman font may
Claim. Sometimes it's not

The people, but a person
I address with his face
Around the corner of
My eye. Take the walls of your

Apartment, or the doors
Between your rooms, while

The subway car passes, and
A tiled vestibule. You fell,

And found a stool, slumped
Onto a silver counter, bent
Between a wall of hot glass
And ice in your wax paper

Cup. You can't hold that for
Long, when all these people
Keep turning like gears
Which lock in the air. It's

Uncanny, I know. Opening
Envelopes filled with
White paper, I look around
And feel the middle of

Each thing unfold. Only
The mountain stays
Me, but there is no
Mountain, like something

Remarkable someone said
When I was in a different
Room. Personae cross
And form what we'd call

A smudge. A little gray-gold
Center, rotted into a voice.

Or turned like that, when
A notepad was bent in half.

There's just no way to see
Without images
Accumulating, without
Hundreds of them flashing

Their availability. Even as
You rush into the street—
There, the angles in
The crosswalks. It's a city

Full of the bank's blue
Awning, which lifts from
Inside its frame. Maybe it's
As simple to remove this

Red box of paper as it is
That faded countertop, but if
One doesn't intend to make
A pile of these things, then

Where do they go? I have
A friend who's taught himself
To recognize people he
Doesn't remember as a kind

Of aggregate person. Maybe
That's not something

He learned. Maybe it's just
Part of what lets him

Forget. That's not me.
I don't walk around
That way. I might lose
The sentence, but

I keep what I was trying to
Say. It turns on me,
And I wish I could push
It off, or take it

Between my fingers,
Make a mark on
The part of my thinking
That's your thinking. Not

The years in decay but
The shifting we move in,
Which I have no
Word for. Not today. This

Occurred to me, and a series
Of voices spilled across
The empty pool in ways
No one could recreate.

## POEM THAT'S NEVER BEEN TO JONES BEACH

I've been at it too long, watching how the ice cubes
are ordered. A cold turn. A touch
on our fingers like knobs are pulled leaving
a house. A dark house, because it's late. Because
the porch has no railing, perhaps, three chairs
are positioned on the lawn, with
boys in them who the cop cars pass at and after "should
we look in the bag," then the bag turning
from vinyl to leather to open: three sacks. It back. Bring
these things of drugs, a gun, unzip across the northeast,
midwest, west itself, where friends of mine start their
days in sweatshirts with plastic ties. They
twist them, or more often they leave them be. This is
the dream I want to be home. With everyone.
Their silence is not a moment I would waste, but
if you like, we can give it back. There's more
real than the heat breaks one
morning, but it does. It's so satisfying, we can
call it recreation. See, I recreate so
pleasantly I can't help it. Spider webs spread
like playing cards on a billboard, or a pile of billboards
leans against some shape. See these trash piles I've been
building. See me cover the table with ice cubes.
I can tell what it is I want to do, and I'm sorry
but I have no other truth. I would like the room.
I would like the time, and to see straight through.

# TWO

## DESCEND, DESCEND

I watched from bed
as it came down loose dust
fell from branches
rained loose down down from the demolition
a day
ago was that building
where there
I point toward what's boom boom boom there now
boom boom boom it's open

a lot of a
disaster an after
wind rock water
down down this isn't that this is before you
even
think a city one way
changes
how it's different when you're aware which is
harder falling building

takes forever
and is supposed to but
I feel like I
have begun to stumble everywhere the
sidewalks
are devastated by
planning
or complexities like traffic somewhere
already I have to


get to and won't
know if I'm going to
in time get there
in the dust falls loosened fell more dust from
branches
like fingers with extra
fingers
the branches hold in branches the dust from
all this enough too much

                    at once we go
down down city center
                    where enough is
          happening so we wait places too much
                    we wait
for things to happen for
                                   enough
          a lot I have not slept a lot lately
I have been looking for


                    an improvement
notice capacity
                    observation
          I have to say I notice description
                    could be
improved a lot I said
                    you have
          to practice at a lot I said you need
to say more notice more

like it's pleasure
to move like it's pleasure
to remain still
in each instance we believe a pleasure
exists
we must ever enjoy
each non
contingent like crème de la crème crème de
crème crème de la crème crème


la crème crème de
la crème crème de la crème
signage on Bell
window signage window city so like
a mall
I enjoy it for its
nineteen
ninety four its lettering that falls from
its era down a thought

like myself when
I stumble over things
lines look up the
lines full of construction clatter debris
airborne
lines opening out of
themselves
like a cloud we were watching too closely
to see they were building

I watched the whole
time I was in bed the
whole time I was
awake I thought I should get out I went
to State
and Caroline I went
to sketch
three courthouse like they were courthouses
built in three different

eras I ask
how the early nineties
era differs
from the era ten years later when put
in terms
of public structures is
a gut
feeling enough I have here a feeling
in place of a gut look


wherein there might
be something more tucked in
back another
asks are we ourselves implicated in
bluish
flowers blooming out of
nowhere
across our lawns as they fill unfolded
tables a neighborhood

barbeque back
driveways back lawns a sprawl
with hoses and
sprinkler attachments which throw mist in mist
a din
of water could there be
a din
of water that's what it would be it's us
who have too much at once

it's us our stuff
falls everywhere at once
I can't hold up
all of what's in my arms yet close the trunk
I can
then fumble into with
my foot
and hip the vestibule one could leave here
bags a moment bags

which I rush with
pressed between my door
and chest and burst
inside bags dropping bags across the floor
I leave
them the living room for
hello
with my hand kitchen counter drinking glass
of water what were you


watching now I
realize I can't quite
remember was
a different building across the street
or trees
further a furniture
store is
collapsing or being built the kind of
place we never think of

                    walking into
and then we're there lying
                    on mattresses
          or trace the racks of sample material
                    high rows
suspended by
                    ceiling
          wires maybe carpet maybe drapes or
simply cloth for covers


                    further there's more
city glass concrete concrete glass
                    where boom boom boom
          opens another window someone is
                    slicing
up vegetables or
                    sitting
          in the part of the night where you have no
idea how you again

will fall asleep
with everything in
motion in a
way more complicated than the spinning
one grows
used to the growth itself
begins
to grow that sort of thought is just what leads
to that sort of you know


you can go back
to bed even if you
don't understand
what you'll do there soon you won't be able
to say
you lay awake for hours
or woke
at points without knowing you had slept is
another part of rest

# THREE

## TOURISM

I think I think of what I want en masse,
as concrete thinks it wants the overpass—

while wind and broken glass want heavy rains,
Los Angeles I want across the plains.

I hear myself collecting what I've caught,
like "in the hospital and you've been shot."

As time so clearly in the precinct falls,
with phone calls mounting crisis on the walls,

police are humming parts of prime-time hooks:
I want their fade-out lines and distant looks.

I want this pickup idling for a beat,
then turning, backing quickly up the street.

I want the time it takes the sound to reach
across from where the tires this moment screech.

I think I often, eyes half-closed, will veer;
I want inside the truck or walking near.

I want the pillow I passed absently,
not wind holding a bag against a tree.

I think I'm in a transformation mood.
I'm going to the diner for some food.

I asked for coffee, but it's not been brought.
I think I've seen this menu quite a lot.

As children love to turn in spinning doors,
I keep rerunning these Formica floors,

though each time through I see there less to take.
I want the leaves from neighbors' trees to rake.

The grass across the street is overgrown.
This was a scene for several years I'd known.

Something I saw there right before it burst.
It's darker later than it was at first.

## FIGURE 5

white lipped
overtly a furnace

two lines tied
the feature on

two screens
you start them

"after a while
it was a quarry

the white walls"
no subject but

a little rings out
in speech or

some circles of
electrics smoke

a scene with
the motors out

taken not left
turned a white

over you see
it touches

## TO MOVE THE CROWD

not where we went,     but set, set for
we bore, we      bore, sat
where we went,         came, we came
then did, dug,   poured, mixed,
prayed, and set, we      flowed, borne,
stained, mauled,       we crowded,
cried, slaughtered,      slain
as if poured,     cried as if
sat, keep         should we hear how
we came cast and left, urged, cried
we art come, cam'st    we slept, then fell,
as we sought,    we bid remember as
we heap, we set       then as we swung,
came not where      we beat, nor knew,
spoke not to stand,     leave, stepped, said shalt
to lose we came      to lie as we mean

## SOME MEASURE OF OUR AFTERMATH

The wetland reeds are under reeds
        we pass across a bridge
Where people sleep unboarded boats
        against abutments ridge

These jetties strike my addled sense
        and edging veins my face
These jetties miles of menace low
        these clutches gear and race

The wheel we hold the rack in line
        the trees we find all burn
The evening shift is over now
        the morning right in turn

We count the threads but not when if
        they're split they rub our skin
And how could we be home if when
        we haven't slipped slept in

Are we far now from Montrose us
        are we now far from where
We pick the burning cinders up
        and scatter them the air

**TOURING FILL**

first a Tuesday while the hour pours
into circles by the statue of Scot under
pink flowers second two tractors pull
raking machines across the beach
green tractors with wide lights
a walkway third where a black storm is
over the river past the overhang and
light rain three feet away makes
a line where there already is grass
and stone fourth a river reflection
a barn with a flag across it fifth
a can of soup in a pot on the stove
the burner on but before it gets hot
sixth under the spider webs mist on
the front porch seventh the house
the end table with green tickets slid from
an envelope used a wrinkle a window

## FENWAY COURT

I take part—as lakes support
        our treading in them—and I possess
even the choice that's made
           for me. PLAY

the open field to sketches a street,
        forward city around them
fell: a line of awnings,
           brick and brown,

garbage flaking where you don't see,
        then you see.
I take to it, what isn't mine:
           I watch its breath.

Its men (two men) dressed as cops.
        They enter the museum
after midnight. I want to say I'm three.
           Rembrandt's *Storm*

is titled *on the Sea of Galilee.*
        I'm late to this art,
that book pile behind me
           so much catches up

I'll never get in place. Too far
        afield to find against,
or between. I can tell the time
           they caught Whitey Bulger

passes from the paintings
          returned does not come.
Speculations settle into
                    books, film. Against

circles, circles raise
          marginal as this F.B.I., and this
I.R.A. Ted Kennedy dead,
                    and a painting cut is

rolled, unrolled: so the wrong ones
          can't find it, so can't get saved—
Saint Mark's remains, smuggled
                    under pork and cabbage,

a Venetian feast—or rather, the heist
          to beat. Providence's Federal Hill
holds out no mystery
                    here is a mystery.

Cities on hills. You find a thing of light
          in your hand not peaceful—
*The Concert*, 1658-1660.
                    On airplanes, in hospitals

the oxygen masks descend into
          our hands. We catch their straps
around a path that won't
                    complete. I'm at a buzzer,

a finger in the inch, half
        an inch, there.
I know the nails on my toes,
           my teeth, and all the skin

in between. It is me—
        unlike anything I've read.
There's the part we know:
          two cops buzz and are

let in, they approach the guard
        station, they ask the other guard
to come downstairs. They act
          like cops, threatening.

We can assume they were afraid,
        the guards as well,
but we know it doesn't matter.
          Taped and bound in

the basement, it doesn't matter.
        That they left no evidence.
That the art can't sell,
          its ruined flakes unfold.

A belilaced cellar hole closes
        like a thunderclap—
a dent in Holland—one
          turn of gunpowder set on

gunpowder, and then not at all:
       *A View of Delft*—
staggers with white trees—*After*
           *the Explosion.* This is

Vermeer joins the guild,
       then an incompleteness
nowhere particular. Its mist
           struck constant like debt.

Like thunderclap. Like out of all
       his view too much,
this, edging back,
           thins under the scene.

Turbo comes into the room
       as we catch the fringe of
what he's moved to
           another subject, sorts

a gangster in Hartford with the bay
       of an auto shop, cooking
on Franklin Avenue, the South End
           is fringe enough.

What's dealt as recovery, amnesty
       is a check paid out
across a low-rent office park, strip-
           mall without stores,

where not enough accumulates again
           to meet you on the front steps
with how many days in that
           shirt, the blood taste

over your lip—beyond your shoulders:
           posts, a set of lawn furniture,
neighbors' porches, and the next
           strewn outward like

a country. Take the book pile
           around my bed, the screens
left open, light in the laundry
           room, garage light:

out from the focus the focus
           recedes. Let's make everything
two Rembrandts, or a Vermeer
           with two paintings hung

beside the open harpsichord, the lid
           decorated, painted, I don't know
the man's face from the lowered
           eyes of his companions.

We don't assume it's more than
           trivia, good trivia—as the cracks
work in before that acid
           feeling, walking ten miles

the sun too pavement to be dangerous,
         sought for more than these
Caravaggios in the Atheneum:
                  Hartford's loan from Rome


given for the Wadsworth returning
         a stolen painting, nothing more
than a summer weekday, walked in
                  half for water, then black


blast of light—strange and tall before
         some death of Christ—the cake
breaks off down the middle of our
                  back, shoulders rotate out


or feet lifting from it's repeated, a long
         time between when we notice
and when we notice. I've shed again,
                  but my preferences steal right


around me: cool there. "You have to keep
         looking"—says the art detective,
his body falling apart
                  on the platform, a person


out of a book I read faded into a film
         I saw, both of them are lost:
we can watch him keep
                  after all the paintings;

the paintings aren't even the art
   I want to catch up to
where I started from. I take a long way
    from lying under

the hammock, a yellow walkman—
   these waters and watering place—
with wind off a beach,
    into the woods: a muscle

that isn't there isn't there to
   delight. Inside the house, they're
casting the bell in *Andrei Rublev*
    on a television with a curve,

crackling speakers. I take apart
   myself, and find a box of cords
loosely tied together, then cards,
    each assigned a value:

a simple watercolor tree, bare
   on a hill, where there aren't hills,
a fence with shadows we can
    follow beyond confusion.

# FOUR

## THE PENNSYLVANIA STATION SEQUENCE (1)

There's a naked girl on a red velvet swing
      Or the name of the song they were singing
Stanford White was shot and someone was
      Caulking the joints of the iron-lined tunnel
Under the Hudson where if you can whistle
      Then it means something would you please
Whistle when it means something I could
      Tell you all about the apparently unstable
Man on the train walking without his father to
      The bathroom where the person who
Had just entered forgot to switch the lock
      From vacant to occupied sometimes I think
I like to buy a magazine less for the articles
      And more for the production don't you enjoy
Thinking some things about gloss and laminate
      How their weight presses like newness when
Kept unfolding in one's jacket pocket here
      Let's open it on the opportunity to combine
Detail and feeling through the reductive act
      Of side story as I was saying there's a naked
Girl on a red velvet swing and a number of
      Unpaid debts a murder trial a vast collection
Of antique furniture burning in a warehouse
      Fire or pink marble piled in the Meadowlands
Also there's White's partner Charles McKim
      Yet another who'd never see the station open

## (11)

What you do is gather together the terms
        Beaux-art and concourse under the prospect of
Post office without allowing for the ironic
        Moment like often I find it has to be culture all
The time I find myself tracing the historical
        Terminal but not the post-war clamshell
Monstrous ticketing what sort of meeting is this
        Happening without a moderator or is everyone
Just thinking meeting what meeting I
        Believe I was talking to myself now either
Pass the conditioner or adjust the temperature
        I prefer it where you think it must be too hot
For your face and then you find it isn't as I was
        Saying though had there been a figure such as
Jackie O in 1963 then maybe this discussion
        Would not be happening um excuse me but
I believe there was such a figure well not one
        Saying is it not cruel to let our city die
By degrees stripped of all her proud monuments
        Until there will be nothing left of all her
Roman elegance to inspire our children except
        If they live on the east side but for those of us
Not so inclined to celebrate the Vanderbilt legacy
        By which I mean we propose a return to our
Discussion the Farley Building and what it was
        Someone was speaking to the limits of fantasy

# (111)

There is a girl on the train you understand
     She has been to many different countries
And she believes that wherever she is right
     Then is her home she says to the women
From Mississippi who think she is interesting
     When she asks them if they like shopping
And they do so she tells them they should
     Absolutely go to Thailand with three empty
Suitcases also try Ethiopian food and visit
     Colorado for the lifestyle she says goodbye
To them while getting off in Meriden where
     I think I should have begun with the tunnels
Shifting in the glacial silt like information is
     For a certain kind of poet I imagine the place
They begin despite the later claims of all
     I thought was how to occupy that absence
Which I can claim as well but more like see
     Fucking Jagr's leaving for the Russian league
Which I imagine in combination with the passage
     Of warehouses or warehouse-like offices
Incidentally raises the question if my father is
     A commercial real estate appraiser wouldn't
That change how I feel about some buildings
     Oh you would like him if he was here he would
Not be sitting backwards on the train even if
     It is a decent analogy for temporal experience

## (IV)

I just want to say first that we can imagine it
        Ok fine but what I'm saying is we already know
That right along with how to drink and speak
        Walk around and look it's better than that stop
Imagining a horizontal Grand Central walk in
        I mean from Seventh Avenue right granite
Columns or iron and plate glass the arcade can
        We say it was arrayed with shopfront windows
Travertine shimmering if we can say shimmering
        Oh that's something you're born with or maybe
You learn how there's a way of walking with
        A bottle of water I took from a friend there's a way
Of talking where you don't tell anybody I said
        Woo but I mean the waiting hall I'm talking
The flood right the general waiting hall was so
        Vaulted the facility of cliché falls into actual
Light casting across fluted columns
        And no benches ok this wasn't New Haven
There was nothing to do in it just be glorious
        And wait for the train right I mean that's why
You're going on about this right well actually
        I think that's more what the concourse was for
Platforms under a tarpaulin of glass and steel
        Stairways leading through cut outs in the floor
You know so it looked how do you say the word
        Skyline so it folds down into trains and tunnels

## (v)

I went there all the time but just on the subway
       I mean I saw this woman snorting heroin from
A Dixie cup standing up the middle of the A
       Noon Tuesday smart though in the express gap
Before fifty-ninth this like I was saying on my
       Way to work as a part time landscape design
Whatever and it was easy getting there at noon
       But going home people the waves at one ramp
Down from the station to where the LIRR exit
       Meets the entrance for the A come around it
Straight into so many people it was like a joke
       Like a commercial I mean I had to stop laugh
At it in the spring with this awful smell burst
       Sewage but you can't stop you have to keep
Walking and be ready for I can't even tell you
       Before the doors closed a rat got on the train
Like anybody we rode for a stop our legs raised
       Pulled into Times Square I mean honestly it
Took me longer than it should to realize things
       Weren't where I thought they were you have to
Listen how people talk about it in a way so that
       Maybe the funniest thing I ever said was Yankee
Stadium in response to where are you now on
       The way from Inwood to Greenpoint you have
To know that's what was moving this agreement
       Like the city is an idea I'm already forgetting it

## (VI)

And then it turned out it was about heartbreak
       You have a train moving from a station toward
A station also a sip of scotch you lean your head
       Back against the headrest and guess what bud
Things accumulate we don't just move through
       Time and get there with what we started with
I don't care if you think New York makes you
       Treat a pair of pants like living somewhere
Else you know I never thought that
       Out it was just one of these ideas comes up
From walking around getting the paper and then
       Abandoning the little plan you know turning left
Instead into the park where not really anyone is
       Sitting like it's seven on a Sunday and what are
You doing up outside with all this dismal shit
       The tiny rain that complements the sense it's
A few degrees colder than you thought it was
       And then it turned out you think maybe now
You've started putting the ending in the middle
       Really asking at which point in this you thought
Of having something to say to people that's how
       It started right all somewhere someone diner
Picture this conversation as not in your head but
       Across the table where it didn't seem you were
Getting into anything just talking it turns out you
       Remember it really takes nothing to remember

# (VII)

It's a form of history I said I was receptive to
      That's all or I should say it's really the delivery
What everybody notices without knowing they're
      Noticing it doesn't matter if you can compress
The air in such a way so that the men breathe
      A sigh of oh no wait that wasn't it let's try again
In order to prevent the Hudson from rushing in
      To the tunnel where the men were bolting iron
Rings to iron rings compressed air was pumped
      In by a don't you think it's sort of funny when
People properly pronounce the word research
      There's a line in a song which I often mishear
So pro now becomes pronoun that's the mistake
      I have affection for these sorts of misperceptions
Perhaps it's because my eyes drift apart from each
      Other naturally I lose focus for a moment more
And more often lately it affects my reading of all
      These magazines what am I doing with distraction
As artifice is that it so arbitrary yes but not actually
      Let's continue again there were men working in
The air under the Hudson they had to enter slowly
      Like a submarine descending and the important
Thing to understand is that coming from the other
      Side of the river there were also men working in
These tunnels that were shifting you understand
      These tunnels were going to meet under the river

## (VIII)

And then it was time to acknowledge the closing
       Was waiting behind everything everybody knows
There's no need for orchestration you can fancy
       Up a situation where the outcome is in question
But here look how a condition of its destruction
       Was the station's continued operation that's one
Don't quite have to make sense if it takes place
       Underground scenario a friend of mine wants to
Burn down St. John the Divine you know like in
       A novel or here I have such a similar opportunity
And yet I want the day to go to the beach instead
       To brush the glass out the way and lie down with
A book of lucid criticism in a slightly cold wind
       Or better still I went out yesterday to pay rent
And ended up getting stoned with my neighbor
       Playing with his baby while we watched a series
Of industrial accidents did you know the Court
       House in Milwaukee has this classically imposing
Façade it comes up after the collapse of Big Blue
       Mega-crane that fell into the new Brewers stadium
Killing three people and leaving one Wisconsin
       Building inspector unable to look at home plate
The same how different from Penn Station
       Where everything was yielded to hazard and one
Was free to inspect the processes of demolition
       Or so said a group of weekend photographers

## (IX)

The event scheduled hadn't at the start time
       Begun so there were these people loosely milling
Around the microphone banquet no platform
       Stand what is it host or maybe there's not always
A particular word for a group of something
       Anyway the point is there were people and it had
Gotten much later than it was supposed to be
       Someone making an announcement not coming
Was not something anyone was prepared for
       At present they had been expecting to be noting
How mister yes sir was devoted to the issue
       While others still were thinking to themselves
Quite a moment to happen at such a time
       Was really something except of course that now
It was nothing got it I mean to get it together
       All you need is the right mixture of phone numbers
And telephones most people will listen if you
       Convince them someone is speaking more so for
Speaking in a context like looking from outside
       The interior is what puts handles on the frying
Pan a friend of mine once said in his experience
       People will not recognize references to themselves
Even when we're looking for them we're really
       Looking for someone to stand up and convince us
That they've been handling the thing from the start
       Like such a surprise to find I'm not who I came to see

## (x)

Can you find out why we're standing in the dark
        While dates appear on screen like part of the story
What specific aspect of your emotional experience
        Can you express with articulations of 1910
It's a little something I know it's a little something
        They're asking us back to the office now for a few
More questions like I'm not convinced and you
        Haven't convinced me you understand the lights
Go out on trains and come back on it's not always
        About your choices often it's about what happens
They aren't going to build a statue for this one
        It's a couple of people talking without stopping
Look there's such a thing as the ball crossing
        The goal line because of inertia there's weight
To these trains they aren't some aluminum
        Version of how to talk without consequences
What's central to any story isn't necessarily
        The story you walk away with some vague
Approximation of what you walked in with
        That line sounds a little familiar doesn't it
You know how you pick these things up
        Just by saying them who can remember when
It's like how many people were even in the room
        Where that conversation happened I don't know
But if you or I weren't one of them then why'd
        We repeat what we heard there to everyone

FIVE

## AT THE BREAKWATER

The clarity of the granite, each piece fit, as if it is
Blue, silver, red as somehow the same color
That holds it together. Last night, I stood in the cold
Across the street from a small white house, held
My fingers up against waves of conversation, warm
Light from table lamps, watched people who didn't
Want to go in there, but had forgotten. Listen: where
Is the voice that lets me know I'm more than two
Stations on the same channel, falling in
And out of range? It was today, on the breakwater,
A hello passed with no person walking before me or
Rising behind. Another hello, and a string
Of hunters appeared nestled along the base of the rocks.
The tide low. They held green rifles. There is
A feeling that catches up on me, walking in the heat,
Or after too much coffee. Like the right word
Coming to you, but without the word. I'm afraid,
I think, of that silvery progression, my skin;
Afraid of my spine, the way things blur. An elevator
Door opens, and the parking garage of
A medical center claims you could be anyone.
But you're not. You don't live with a split in
Your throat, some sentence you either can't quite hear or
Can't get said, as you watch yourself from out
On the flats, at a distance, as you shout back now,
Before the tide comes in, while you can still turn home.

## POEM WITH ALL THE TIME IN THE WORLD

We came to love going together
Down the hill into the abandoned corridor
On walks, where hollowed out buildings
Would surround our discussion.

We talked mostly about work, should we
Go another block, some place
For dinner, and oddly, we never brought
Up the feeling that everything

Was on fire, that if we pushed into
A wall, our handprints would remain.
This was before our own neighborhood
Started to disappear—not all at once,

More it was like being unable to find
Yourself excited
By a book for months, an absence
You'd forget and then somehow put

Your tongue to, this topic
That might erupt over too much
Coffee but mostly was unreadable,
Unseen in front of you.

It made us feel so young and fearful
When we'd run into a stranger on
The street. We'd go to ask
What they thought was happening,

Did they also see that it was
Happening, but then we'd dodge at
The last second, whispering
Did they know where this particular

Street was? Oh we're on that street
Now, yes we see the sign there, and oh
How funny, as we walked home,
Turning incessantly over what

Had just happened, how we might be
Different next time—but then
We'd walk out one morning,
And the racks would all be empty

In front of our market, and in front
Of the market around the corner
Where we circled, debating if we
Should ask why there was no fruit.

We got used to it. The way our street
Looked without a single car, how if we
Swept the trash out of the gutters,
they stayed clean. It was a strange time.

We said so openly. Eventually, we said,
Summer ends. We get caught up
Again in our own lives. The leaves
Fall, and trees open into the sky.

## OFTEN, COMMON, SOME, AND FREE

Dear, neither of us has any
money. Let's say
we leave that field open, as in
we don't complete

the form. I see nothing here
says it is required.
Maybe this is the other kind
of field. Grass, etc.

That makes sense to me.
Dear, neither of us has any
money. Let's say
there's an Adirondack chair,

the affordable plastic kind.
Maybe those are rubber.
Maybe I don't know what
rubber is. Me. Forget it,

we know the park is free.
Rather, further, also, trees.
There's a soft line of them. Soft
as in thin and irregular.

The trees themselves are full.
Their shadows cross
our blanket, as in let's say
we have a blanket, which

we move where the sun's
got the same feel to it. Still.
You instruct me: be still.
Dear today. Dear yesterday.

What a lot of places I moved
myself around then.
Again. Sunny afternoons
my father sits in

a plastic Adirondack chair
with his fingers folded
and his shirt open. No one
listens, he doesn't speak.

It's nice he thinks of it
as a privilege, but nicer
still that he does it.
Again. What did I say?

The field is open, as in
incomplete. The grass,
I don't have a word for
except, rather, excuse me,

please. Please,
as in this afternoon,
stay in
the park with me.

## TINNITUS ASKS A QUESTION

Ringing on the street, you know, that day I saw
        a girl on a bike get hit by a pickup—she was
very angry—it was ringing everywhere, it was
        what made me wonder if she was screaming

for someone to go over and say I don't know
        why, but actually, it's ringing everywhere for me
too. Somewhere, the lightning, the clouds, below,
        actually below in the clouds, a lot of lightning:

listen, I'm not always at a loss, like right now, when
        I'm on an airplane—engines ringing—an airplane
on which I'm coming back from California, where
        the beach was near the airport, and other places,

the beach was, for instance, by the train, when
        I was on the train, and those dolphins, can I
mention them, because I was on a train when
        I saw them, forgive me if that's not a good

reason. Sometimes my thinking is you have to
        forget which entree and choose a restaurant:
for a moment, roughly, I'll let that idea be how
        even though no one on this plane could know

where I misplaced a particular picture—the one
        where I'm in the room I can't remember where
was—and though I can't reasonably expect a useful
        answer, I have to think I might remember more

by asking. By accident. By knocking. By a bell.
By touching the side of a bell again. By again
again. By walking out the door. By not expecting
those trees suddenly to have flowers again.

By we know what day it was, by where we were,
the lightning, flying, what made me frightened,
more than on a plane or it is ringing, was asking
how can I know in here if it's ringing enough.

## BLACK HELICOPTERS

There are categories of people I don't fall
        into and while I'm unsure of the reason for
it being important, I've been paying attention
        so I know it's true. Like I knew, the other

night, when two SUVs skidded into position,
        blocking off my street, that after they left,
a helicopter would still be circling. There are
        people who haven't seen that and I know

how it looks when I say don't count me
        among them. But I pay attention, so when
a gloved hand throws spikes across the road
        before the runaway jeep gets there, I can

turn my head before it hits. I wanted to look
        away is an excuse for not having to say if
this really happened. Today's reason for not
        knowing why something is good is no

better than today's reason for not knowing
        why something isn't. And then, a change.
Earlier I made a statement that amounts to
        how things can be enough by being

cinematic is a way some people felt and I
        was one of them. Now, different, I move
from believing that men, out of the dark, are
        spiraling down on thick, metallic rope,

to believing in what they are spiraling for.
　　　　　As in, it might not be enough to prove
a mystery exists if it doesn't mean anything
　　　　to your life. Or does that complicate

needlessly what's just me asking myself
　　　　　do you really have to be chased across
a gravel rooftop in order to not fall off?
　　　　　Then maybe in the end it's best to

focus less on whether the black boots
　　　　　crashing through bedroom windows,
themselves, are good or bad, and more
　　　　　on what could we need them to be here

for? Rather, here still? That question.
　　　　　What makes people return to tension.
Let's ask if we can change the ending
　　　　　so that not seeing helicopters meaning

they are there, as an idea, becomes not
　　　　　seeing them because they never were.
Let's say we don't need them. Though
　　　　　we're the kind of people who often do.

## OH STEREO

I don't know how it goes.
What I had was humming
a little bit. That almost
feeling. I suspected those

days, I was always talking
about the same thing,
and I intended to change
the subject, even

though there were some
people I didn't like
around. This was when
the weather, I'd often

notice, had been
approaching. It was
like coming to at
a party. Or several.

Always with the feeling
I should've rather
ended up out in
their backyard ably

breaking something like
stairs. Folks
trigger the light
sensor, came to smoke,

weaved in and out
of my time there. I mean
I was tired. All this
trying to stay

up was putting me to
sleep. Outdoors
in the rain. Noticing
I left some notebook

open, except I didn't
use a notebook. Also,
I was sitting there,
writing how it's more

humming. Now
you hum with me. We
can do the middle
of the road, a car

idling by a curb,
a paper bag caught
under a tire, someone
parked on the wrong

side, left their door
open. In there, they've got
songs on, finally—
what everything was

screaming for. I don't
know what time is
here. I mean I don't
keep time. Kindness,

I notice, when you like
didn't want to hum
with me, do anyway,
would still. I appreciate

enough. How a good
thing doesn't exactly
have to happen.
We're moving that way.

## POEM IN WHICH MY LOVE WILL NOT LET YOU DOWN

*Hold still.* And that was all we said,
       Having found shadows on the porch, warm
In places that should've been cool still,
       Places that had stayed dark all day. It was
The same when we filled the tub with

       Cool water—we tried it, with our hands
Up to our wrists, and it was seawater, warm
       In the tub when we had just woken up. Or
It woke us, the tub filling with seawater—
       And that was a dream we were having:

One where seawater fills the tub. Maybe
       Then we thought this is how to live now.
With the thing as we feared it. Or we said
       *Hold still.* I said it, and then you said it.
We said it together, like it was our breath.

       Then we were in Rome again. Walking
In a crowd from one dark field into
       Another. You shouted *Via Appia!* And so
I shouted *Via delle Capannelle!* Gianfranco
       Shouted *Via Appia e Via delle Capannelle!*

And we shouted into the plastic phone
       *Via Appia or Via delle Capannelle!* This was when
We were walking so close I saw faces
       In the back of the man before me, buzzing
In places, I was numb still in others

From the concert, from jumping in place,
From being thirsty, from drinking water. All of
These lines of rope and if you crossed them
People shouted. We shouted *Is this your car!*
And we shouted *Are you the person I am*

*Speaking to! Am I speaking to you!* And then
We had our heads against the headrests,
Driving too fast, it seemed because of the music—
I wasn't driving but it was how I would
Drive because of the music, and in the past,

When it felt like I was in several cities at
Once (with you), or in places that weren't cities,
Never would be. The air rose as far as
The mountains. It held. And shadows were
Everywhere, but there was nothing

We couldn't see through. The highway
Interchanges pile atop each other, in rings that
Breathe. It was the sky over Texas,
And we chased the reach of our fingers
With roads. Out where we couldn't even tell

If the air was hot, it was too full of
Direction. It was what we wanted. To be in
A vagueness specific, like the name
Of a wind. The sky was not red.
It was gray, then black, then dimly blue.

We sat in the waves on the shore, in
       Thick Florida sand, or we stood on stones
At an Adriatic beach with water so
       Cold it was like a dream. Something
You'd have to make up, but wouldn't

       Know how. Wouldn't have known
You had to. Or we are in your place.
       Springsteen and us. Over us.
Over the couch, and the short table.
       Filling in the lamplight in the corner,

And the choice to lie down on a rug,
       To lay out a game between us,
And listen, as the trees in Houston turn
       Their branches against windows
In Montrose, on Hawthorne Street,

       Listen, as the song goes *In the silence,*
*I hear my heart beating,* and then *time*
       *Slipping away.* Hear it repeat.
We play it again, and it pours around
       Us into whatever room we keep.

NOTES

Robert Moses served as the New York City Parks Commissioner, chairman of the Triborough Bridge and Tunnel Authority, and head of the New York State Parks Council, among a number of other positions. The bathhouses of Jones Beach, the Astoria, Crotona, McCarren, Sunset and Hamilton Fish Park pools, the West Side Highway, the Cross-Bronx Expressway, and the Triborough Bridge make up a small number of the public works for which he was responsible. The Brooklyn-Battery Bridge does not.

"Descend, Descend" is set in Houston, TX.

"Figure 5" is after the painting by Jasper Johns.

"To Move the Crowd" takes its verbs from the first of Ezra Pound's *Cantos*.

"Some Measure Of Our Aftermath" alludes to Jehanne's repeated question, "Dis, Blaise, sommes-nous bien loin de Montmartre?" from Blaise Cendrars's *La prose du Transsibérien et de la Petite Jehanne de France*.

Thirteen works of art, including Vermeer's *The Concert* and Rembrandt's *Storm on the Sea of Galilee* and *A Lady and Gentleman in Black*, were stolen by a pair of thieves from the Isabella Stewart Gardner Museum in the Fenway on March 18, 1990.

On the destruction of the original Pennsylvania Station, from the

October 30, 1963 New York Times: "It's not easy to knock down nine acres of travertine and granite, 84 Doric columns, a vaulted concourse of extravagant, weighty grandeur, classical splendor modeled after royal Roman baths, rich detail in solid stone, architectural quality in precious materials that set the stamp of excellence on a city. But it can be done."

The 2,500-ft-long rubble mound breakwater in Provincetown Harbor was constructed from 1970-1972 out of approximately 328,000 tons of stone.

## ACKNOWLEDGMENTS

Thanks to the editors of the journals where versions of these poems previously appeared: *American Poetry Review:* "Black Helicopters"; "Poem That's Never Been To Jones Beach"; "Poem With All the Time In the World"; *Ampersand Review:* "Figure 5"; *Bennington Review:* "At the Breakwater"; *Better:* "Oh Stereo"; *Bomb:* "To Move the Crowd"; *Cannibal:* "The Pennsylvania Station Sequence"; *Colorado Review:* "Advanced Fantasies Of the Cross-Bronx Expressway"; "Visionary Labors Of the Astoria Pool"; *Cream City Review:* "Some Measure Of Our Aftermath"; *Driftless Review:* "The Pennsylvania Station Sequence" (reprint); *jubilat:* "At McCarren Pool"; *Lana Turner:* "Touring Fill"; *The Nation:* "Sunset Pool"; *The New Yorker:* "Poem For the Opening Of the Hamilton Fish Park Pool, 1936"; "Tourism"; *Octopus:* "Descend, Descend"; *A Public Space:* "Tinnitus Asks a Question"; *Ploughshares:* "Often, Common, Some, And Free"; *Poetry:* "A Partial View Of the Triborough"; "The Brooklyn-Battery Bridge In the Brooklyn-Battery Tunnel"; "Poem Which Wants To Be Called the West Side Highway"; *Poetry Northwest:* "Poem In Which My Love Will Not Let You Down"; "*The Volta:* "Fenway Court."

This book was written, and then re-written, over many years. I'd like to thank my classmates and teachers from the University of Houston, where many of these poems began, as well as my colleagues and graduate students at the University of South Carolina, who have supported and inspired me as I finished this work. I am grateful to all the friends, poets, teachers, editors, and family who have read and responded to these poems over the years, and I especially would like to thank Rusty Morrison, Ken Keegan, and everyone at Omnidawn for finding a place for this book and for bringing it out to the world.

## ABOUT THE AUTHOR

Samuel Amadon is the author of *Like a Sea, The Hartford Book,* and *Listener.* His poems have appeared in *The New Yorker, The Nation, Poetry, American Poetry Review, Kenyon Review,* and *Lana Turner.* He is the winner of the 2013 Believer Poetry Book Award, and he directs the MFA Program in Creative Writing at the University of South Carolina. With Liz Countryman, he edits the poetry journal *Oversound.*

*Often, Common, Some, And Free*
Samuel Amadon

Cover art: "Dark Duck," oil on jute, 94 x 68 inches, by Spencer Lewis, 2018
Photography by Ruben Diaz, courtesy of the artist

Cover typefaces: Tribute and Scala sans
Interior typefaces: Scala with Tribute and Scala sans

Cover and interior design by adam b. bohannon

Printed in the United States
by Books International, Dulles, Virginia
On 55# Glatfelter B19 Antique
Acid Free Archival Quality Recycled Paper

Publication of this book was made possible in part by gifts from
Katherine & John Gravendyk in honor of Hillary Gravendyk,
Francesca Bell, Mary Mackey, and The New Place Fund

Omnidawn Publishing
Oakland, California
Staff and Volunteers, Fall 2021

Rusty Morrison & Ken Keegan, senior editors & co-publishers
Kayla Ellenbecker, production editor & poetry editor
Rob Hendricks, editor for *Omniverse*, marketing, fiction & post-pub publicity
Sharon Zetter, poetry editor & book designer
Liza Flum, poetry editor
Matthew Bowie, poetry editor
Anthony Cody, poetry editor
Jason Bayani, poetry editor
Gail Aronson, fiction editor
Laura Joakimson, marketing assistant for Instagram & Facebook, fiction editor
Ariana Nevarez, marketing assistant & Omniveres writer, fiction editor
Jennifer Metsker, marketing assistant